# *Bent Not Broken*

Kathleen Downing Melillo

**Bent Not Broken**
**Copyright © 2016 Kathleen Downing Melillo.** Produced by Stillwater River Publications. All rights reserved. No part of this publication may be reproduced, distributed, or transmitted in any form or by any means, including photocopying, recording, or other electronic or mechanical methods, without the prior written permission of the publisher or author, except in the case of brief quotations embodied in critical reviews and certain other noncommercial uses permitted by copyright law. Written and produced in the United States of America.

Visit our website at **www.StillwaterPress.com** for more information.

First Stillwater River Publications Edition

ISBN-10: 0-692-69992-9
ISBN-13: 978-0692-69992-8

1 2 3 4 5 6 7 8 9 10

Written by Kathleen Downing Melillo
Original Cover Art by Kristin Patto Blake
Cover & Interior Design by Dawn M. Porter
Published by Stillwater River Publications, Glocester, RI, USA.

*The views and opinions expressed in this book are solely those of the author and do not necessarily reflect the views and opinions of the publisher.*

# DEDICATION

*This book is dedicated to all
who have suffered heartache, heartbreak, or loss,
yet have remained bent, not broken.*

# PRELUDE

One road
Revealing multiple paths
When chosen wisely
Are filled with potential:
Hopes,
Dreams, happiness...
Every day
Is a new beginning
A fresh start,
An empty page
Ready to be written,
Acted out:
Lived...
Choices,
Actions,
Interactions,
And inactions as well
Become the text
In what will become
The next chapter,
Yesterday's memories,
Tomorrow's hope and dreams,
It's your future...
Choose wisely

*I'll begin at the end  
The beginning of our decline  
When I first realized  
My own life I had to find.  
Although my story begins with the end of my marriage,  
the story of my marriage you won't hear.  
My story focuses on hope, faith, prayer,  
and the importance of keeping friends and family near...*

*A decline is a decline,  
Life's circumstances may change  
but the end result  
is always the same.  
I'm thinking you'll identify  
with all I have to say,  
and agree,  
no matter your life's circumstances,  
if there's a will, there's a way...*

## CROSSROADS

There's sadness in my heart
It's running out of control
It's taken over my life
I don't know which way to go.

I feel like I'm at a crossroad
And I'm not sure which road to choose
However, I'm certain,
No matter which way I go,
Someone will lose.

It really comes down to
Do I choose for them or for me
I never truly understood
How difficult a decision this would be.

Every night and day
This weighs heavily upon my heart
Should I stay and do what's right
Or be the one to tear my family apart.

They are beginning to notice
I haven't been quite the same
Although no one's really sure why
They look to each other with blame.

*They're looking for the reason
But what they cannot see:
It's got nothing to do with them,
It's what's missing inside of me.*

*My life is a good one,
My family's the best,
Maybe this is God
Putting me to the test.*

*I've always been a good person,
Daughter, mom, and wife
It just seems there's something more;
Like I'm missing something in my life.*

*While searching for the answer
I've locked myself inside
I don't talk about my feelings
And surprisingly, haven't cried.*

*To others it's always appeared*
*That I'd always had it all*
*Loving husband and beautiful family*
*My life was just a ball.*

*I guess that's exactly*
*What I wanted others to believe*
*But I'm not truly happy*
*And no longer want to deceive.*

*Now that it's out in the open*
*There's a decision I have to make*
*Yet I still stand at the crossroads*
*Now knowing which road to take.*

Kathleen Downing Melillo

*After teetering on the crossroads
between where I wanted and needed to be,
The lies came full circle
Making my path so very clear to me.*

## THE CHOSEN ROAD

*A weight has been lifted*
*The pressure is gone*
*I've chosen my path*
*My independence is born.*
*My mood has been altered*
*My vision has cleared*
*The decision was easier than I thought*
*The pain was much less than I feared.*
*Everything came to a head*
*When I learned of all the lies*
*I packed up all of our bags*
*And severed all ties.*
*I didn't question myself*
*And I never looked back*
*I did look toward my future*
*As I began to unpack.*
*My kids are OK*
*They've adjusted quite well*
*I've taught them to handle things*
*And never ever to dwell.*

*Their dad is their dad*
*As he will always be*
*The only difference is*
*He's no longer a part of me.*
*We are being very civil*
*As civil as a separation can be*
*We want to model good behavior*
*For the girls are watching us closely.*
*What we want to teach them,*
*What it is we are trying to convey*
*Is that we can still be friends*
*Even after going our separate ways.*
*And in the end*
*What I would like to see*
*Is although we're living*
*Our lives separate*
*We still act like a family.*

*Divorce;
separation,
dissociate,
split-up,
break up,
distance,
detach,
disconnect...
No matter
the word choice
the meaning
remains
the same,
as does
its affect
on all
parties involved;
the termination
of a family,
the conclusion
of a life once shared,*

*the shutting down
of emotion,
feeling,
caring,
concern,
the end
of
togetherness,
contentment,
happiness,
a bond,
a unit,
what is stable,
and familiar...
The beginning
of the uncertain;
the unknown...*

*Then began not a new chapter*
*But a new book about me*
*Who knew then*
*What a rollercoaster ride*
*It would be.*

*There were many days*
*that I felt so all-alone*
*But because I had two girls to raise*
*Weakness could not be shown.*

*I did what I had to do*
*As I started over from scratch*
*To get out of the hole I was left in*
*A break I couldn't seem to catch.*

*I held my head high*
*And faced all my fears*
*To others I was a warrior*
*they never saw my tears.*

## MASKS

*No one wants to walk around
wearing their vulnerabilities
on their sleeves.
We adorn masks
to hide behind,
a front,
a façade;
camouflage.
We want to blend in
with what is
"normal."
The mask I wear
is called
"strength."
I want others,
and myself as well,
to see me as being
strong, resilient, and independent.
What I don't want to display
is weakness.
I hide behind my strength
so others won't see
that I too have weaknesses,
that I am unsure about my path
and my choices.*

*I don't want them to see me cry
as I struggle along my path
of uncertainty;
to cry for what I have lost,
to cry for what I can no longer
provide for my children.
Instead
I want to see myself
and be seen
for all that I choose to celebrate,
all the positives that are in my life,
all that I can control.
I want them to see
that life's circumstances
may lead me
into unchartered territories,
places filled with darkness and despair,
but life's circumstances
can only defeat me
if I allow them.
I choose to live my life,
my way,
and enjoy every step along the way
with a smile.*

*Thank God for my family
And friends that truly cared
Cuz they looked out for me
As I faced the world feeling alone and scared.*

*Friends
are the soul mates
that makes life
worth living...
Always
in the corners
of our minds...
An unbreakable bond,
connection,
a familiarity
to fall back upon...
Perpetual
open doors
we are able
to walk
in
and out of
during
our lifetime...
Always there
always willing
listening,*

*sharing,
loving,
caring...
forever
in our hearts...
Thank you my friends,
my soul mates,
for being
the wonderful people
you are
and for sharing
in my life
yesterday,
today,
tomorrow,
always and forever.
Thank you my friends,
my soul mates
for being
the wonderful people
you are
and for sharing
in my life
yesterday,
today,
tomorrow,
always and forever.*

*Girlfriends, wing-women*
*you might say*
*know all the rules*
*and are always ready to play.*
*And when you get together*
*nothing else exists*
*and the last thing you'll think of*
*is your lack of wedded bliss...*

*Wingman*
*Knows the plan of action,*
*prepares for liftoff,*
*follows the plan,*
*knows the signals,*
*and never, ever,*
*abandons.*
*Takes a hit*
*in order to save;*
*no matter*
*how hard the hit!*
*Takes the controls*
*whenever*
*control is*
*broken, altered, lost*
*or*
*simply*
*recklessly abandoned.*
*In charge of*
*relationship challenged,*
*those in a commitment,*

*or  
those in need  
of being committed!  
One who is  
behind you 100%  
no matter  
what you say;  
it's your story  
and they're  
sticking to it...  
Properly prepared  
for search and destroy  
upon a moment's notice  
prompted by  
a simple word  
or look.  
Goes into battle  
and  
goes down in flames.*

*It's all fun and games
when troubles are off your mind
however, a string of carefree days
is very hard to find.*

*Then you have those days
not even yourself you can con
the weight of the world's on your shoulders
and you've got to convince yourself to go on...*

*Some days
there's a spring in your step
and a swagger in your stride
where the world's your oyster
and there's no stopping you.
While others days
you can't find the strength
to move an inch,
and you have no dreams;
everything looks bleak
except crawling back in bed.
Never accept defeat,
don't give into
the darkness
that is luring you
into its lair.
You have the power
to look darkness
in the eye
and choose
to look toward the light,
the positive,
the optimistic,*

*and
find the confidence
to conquer
the demons
that seek
the weak,
the fragile,
the tired.
Find your strength,
to overcome the negativity
that breeds in darkness
from these demons.
Fear feeds off the weak
but
cannot thrive in the light;
in strength.
Believe in your strength,
shine your light,
defeat the darkness
with your power.*

*And with every stumble
along your way
you continue to remind yourself
tomorrow's a new day.*

*All the steps
you have taken
in your journey of life
have led you
to where you are today
and have helped
make you
the wonderful person
you have become.
Yesterday
is a memory
to be savored,
not simply left behind.
Today lies before you,
with each step
and every choice
yours to make;
your future to chart.
Each advance,
whether big or small
is filled with  opportunities.*

*Live and enjoy every moment
to its fullest
whether advances are minimal
or vast.
Never wish the time away,
for tomorrow will arrive
with new choices & possibilities
and will be filled with
memories of each & every yesterday
linked together in a slideshow
for you to visit,
to pick and choose
at your whim.
Just remember
that yesterdays are filled with steps
that you've taken,
steps that can be seen,
but never changed or retraced.
May today be a gift
you'll always treasure
and know that
you can build a new tomorrow
even if the past still aches.*

*Although I was moving forward
and making progress along my way
it never took away the pain
it simply held it at bay...*

*All the hurt inside
acts on its own accord
building walls around me,
around the happiness
that awaits
somewhere out there
longing to find me.
I've closed every door
to keep everyone at bay,
now I can no longer see
the light,
only the darkness that dims
all of my days.
Days come and go
and life passes
as I simply
go through the motions
of my bane existence.
Dreams are a distant memory
only nightmares remain.*

Kathleen Downing Melillo

*This roller-coaster ride
won't slow down
long enough
for me to escape,
it speeds along
tracks unknown,
trapping me,
frightening me.
Although I live in fear
I am fighting
for survival,
gaining strength,
seeking and planning
my escape.
My life,
my hopes,
my dreams,
are worth more.
This ride cannot keep me,
I am stronger
than the sum
of all my fears...*

*Our life wasn't all doom and gloom
we had many laughs along the way
thanks again to family and friends
we learned to enjoy ourselves I must to say.*

*If it were up to me
I wouldn't have taken chances
walked the straight and narrow
without giving options second glances.*

*The unsure
the unknown
you'll never know
until you've been shown.
It's trusting what you think
and going with what you feel
that will lead you to what's right
and true happiness that's surreal.
For you'll never know
if you hide behind the walls
throw away the mortar and bricks
take a breath, leap, and stand tall.
If you make a mistake
take it in stride
cuz you lived and you learned
and know that you tried.
If something's worth having
then it's worth losing
you just have to know
what's worth choosing.
Pick and choose your battles
it's a jungle out there
when it's worth the fight
then it's obvious you care.
Keep the faith
and your head held high
accept the hand of fate
and never question why.*

*Never be afraid
happiness isn't over when you lose
it's over when you quit
the dream is yours to choose.*

*I did learn a lot
about what is meant to be
if it's not we can't force it
it just took a while to become clear to me.*

*We can chase our dreams*
*and work toward our goals*
*but what's meant to be will be*
*as our lives effortlessly unfold*
*We can try to force what isn't*
*what wasn't meant to be*
*but in the end*
*we must accept our fate, our destiny*
*We can look for signs*
*while we work and play*
*that guide us where we want to be but no matter how*
*hard we try*
*what's truly meant to be will always find its way*
*So if one day you find yourself*
*on a road you'd never imagined you'd be*
*you'll know deep in your soul*
*that's where you're meant to be*
*So accept your fate*
*and smile each and every day*
*the universe is smarter than you*
*and God has a master plan anyway.*

*And on those days
I was feeling sorry for myself
feeling my life was cursed
I added a dose of perspective
and remembered my life could be worse.*

*Life doesn't always go as planned*
*things aren't always as they appear*
*some days are the shit*
*and life's a pain in the rear.*
*No matter what you do*
*or how hard you try*
*nothing goes right*
*and you continuously sigh.*
*Your spirit is broken*
*your will is running dry*
*all you want to do*
*is hang your head and cry.*
*Tomorrow is another day*
*a chance to start anew*
*try to keep your chin up*
*you're not the only one who's blue.*
*Get over yourself*
*be glad you're alive*
*the chance for one more day*
*is for what others strive.*
*So when you see life as not half full*
*but a half empty cup*
*reach for your crazy straw*
*and suck it up.*

*It's OK to feel sad,*
*when your world's tossed up-side down*
*as you fight between failure and strength*
*and you waft between a smile and a frown.*

*I say I'm strong  
yet I'm very weak  
I say I'm independent  
yet I'm needy  
I say I don't need anyone  
yet I'm afraid of being alone  
I say I'm impervious  
yet I seek the approval of everyone  
I say that I'm brave  
yet I'm frightened beyond belief  
I say that I'm confident  
yet I'm extremely insecure  
I say that I'm powerful  
yet I feel insignificant  
I say I can do it all  
yet I want someone to help  
I show the world a smile  
yet I'm crying inside  
I hold my head up high  
yet I want my burden eased.*

*I want the world to see me
As all of the things
that I want to be
strong
independent
Self-reliant
brave
confident
powerful
and
secure
Please see
who I am
in-between
all that I want
the world to see,
all that I strive
to be...*

*Then there were times*
*Choices weren't clear to see*
*But I know I made the right choices*
*For my kids and me.*

## RIGHT OR WRONG?

*From the moment we're born*
*we were expected to do what was right.*
*Our parents followed all the rules*
*in order to raise the "perfect" child.*
*As soon as we were able to speak,*
*please and thank you were forced upon us*
*as part of our vocabulary.*
*As children, we're expected to behave*
*with certain expectations.*
*always speak kindly to others,*
*be sure to share,*
*never lie, cheat, or steal.*
*We learned, as we grew,*
*that we must accept the choices we make*
*and to act responsible, to do the right thing.*
*The old saying,*
*"you've made your bed, now lie in it,"*

*was tossed about freely.
But, when you think about
decisions you've made
in order to do what's right,
don't you ever wonder,
what is the right thing?
Who is the right thing 'right' for?
Suppose a decision made in the past
is no longer a good decision
in the present?
what's the 'right' thing to do?
Lie in the proverbial bed
you've made for yourself,
no matter how bad it has become;
no matter who suffers,
just to remain a responsible person?
When does making a decision
that is good for now,
going against what is
the 'right' thing to do,
not the wrong thing to do?*

Kathleen Downing Melillo

*A life changing decision*
*is never an easy one to make*
*there's always that stray thought*
*what if I chose the other road to take.*

## **REGRET**

*To feel sorry and sad
about something previously
done or said
that now appears
wrong,
mistaken,
or hurtful
to others...
I try to live
each and every day
without regret,
without
saying or doing
anything
wrong,
mistaken,*

*or hurtful
to others
so I can
wake up
knowing
that the choices
I have made
are of a positive nature
and are
precise,
correct,
or kind
to others..
Always treat others
as you wish
to be treated
and regret
will never inhabit
your mind,
your heart,
or your soul...*

*I never felt sorry for myself
For being left by the side of the road
And I know I'm not alone in my feelings
But I felt my story
Needed to be told.
Some details were left out
some things are better left unsaid
but I'll be honest
at times I thought it would be easier if I were dead.*

## THOUGHTS

*So many thoughts cohabitating
all struggling to reach to the top
each one wanting to surface first
all too strong to be defeated
there are always two sides
to everything
so there's always
the good and the bad
the war between good and bad
constantly rages in my mind
I root for the positive*

*and try to smile
but without watching
I'm blindsided
by an unsuspecting
random thought
a constant reminder
of all that has gone
terribly wrong in my life
not willing to be defeated
by life's circumstances
I force them aside
knowing they're not gone
nor forgotten
simply cast into submission
until they become strong enough, again
until they wear upon my thoughts so heavily
and gain the strength
to resurface
where the war
between good and evil rages
where the victor remains unseen...*

*I did a lot of writing
during those early years
mostly to convince myself
of something
my father once said,
"My faith is stronger than my fears."
My journey was a collaborative effort
of not just my two girls and me
we all grew as strong women
who knew what an amazing adventure it would be.*

*I've come a long way in the past seven years*
*It's been quite the journey*
*I have not traveled it entirely by myself.*
*I've been helped*
*each and every step of the way.*
*First and foremost*
*I have my mom to thank*
*As she opened her door*
*Without hesitation,*
*For my girls,*
*Who supported me each and every step of the way,*
*Whether they agreed with my choices*
*Or not.*
*Next, my brothers and sisters*
*Who encouraged me,*
*And reminded me,*
*That this too shall pass,*
*To have faith and hope,*
*To stay strong,*
*And pray, pray, pray.*
*Then there were my friends,*
*Who were there*
*At a moment's notice, whenever I needed them,*
*Or stood waiting in the wings,*
*For their chance*
*To help me along my path.*
*Finally, my dad,*
*I prayed to him*
*For guidance,*

*To point me in the right direction,
Give me the advice
I so desperately needed,
And to watch over my family
As I struggled
To resurrect our lives
From the ashes
I was left with.
I am where I am
And am the person that I am
Because of each
And every person
That has listened to me,
Comforted me,
Housed me,
Nourished me,
Counseled me,
Let us not forget
Drank with me,
And at times,
Carried me.
I couldn't have accomplished
All that I have
Without each and every person who not only
Touched my life,
But changed it
Forever.*

*I'm finally at a point in my life*
*Where I never dreamed I'd be*
*Because we now live in*
*A beautiful house*
*Purchased by none other than*
*Little ole me.*
*My message to you*
*Is quite simple you see*
*Never accept defeat*
*Or be afraid of what you want*
*and where you want*
*and need to be.*

*Safety,
protection from,
or not being
exposed to,
the risk
of harm
or injury...
Most people
go through life
in their own
parallel universe;
they go through life
with tunnel vision.
Living,
having life,
not dead
or
nonexistent,
alive in name only.
When we fear
the unknown*

*and lead
a nonexistent life;
fear grabs hold,
metastasizes,
and
takes over
our mind,
heart,
body and soul.
It's when we
look fear
in the eye,
dissect,
understand,
and conquer
these fears
that we take
the first step
toward a real life
toward happiness...
and learn,
there's nothing to fear but fear itself...*

*Not everyone will always agree
with every choice you make
and unless they've walked a mile in your shoes
a verbal bashing toward you they shouldn't partake.*

*Does anyone care what I think?*
*Does anyone care how I feel?*
*Does anyone even care about me?*
*Do people feel that*
*they can walk all over me*
*simply because*
*it is in my character*
*to do all I can*
*to please everyone*
*in any way that I can?*
*And, when I speak my mind*
*about something*
*or have an opinion*
*do they realize that it hurts*
*to be looked upon as being*
*ungrateful, difficult, or simply a bitch.*
*All my life*
*I have done for others*
*forsaking myself at times,*
*in order to make them happy,*
*to make their life a little easier,*
*or just to put a smile on their face.*
*Well, I've decided*
*that life is too damn short,*
*and now it's time for me.*
*It's time to do what is right*
*for myself and for my family,*
*time to make my life a little easier,*
*time to make me happy*
*and time put a much-deserved smile*
*upon my face.*

Kathleen Downing Melillo

*Waiting for someone else*
*to make me happy*
*is no longer an option.*
*In order to insure*
*that people no longer disappoint me*
*I will not expect anything from anyone.*
*I have to learn*
*to put my needs first*
*and not concede*
*or accept anything less*
*than all that I want*
*and truly deserve out of life;*
*that which makes me truly happy.*
*I choose to begin living for me.*
*I am no longer living my life*
*always worrying about*
*what others think,*
*what they need,*
*what they want,*
*or how they feel.*
*No one seems to understand*
*that I have needs as well*
*and I simply refuse*
*to continue to give*
*to those*
*who do not respect the fact*
*that I am only human,*
*I am not perfect,*
*and that I too*
*need to feel*
*that someone is there*
*for me.*

*Now's the time to set yourself a goal
Never settle for anything less
Than all you want and deserve in life
No matter how big the mess.*

## Kathleen Downing Melillo

Each day in life is an adventure
Every turn of the page unknown
So enjoy every minute to its fullest
Whether with loved ones or all alone.

Always wear a smile upon your face
It shows the beauty within
Smiles are very contagious
And are passed to others on a whim.

These smiles are positive and encouraging
On even our darkest days,
They give us hope and promise
And remind us of better days.

So when you're feeling low,
Just know you're not alone
Remember, this too shall pass,
Focus on the positive vs. the unknown.

Worry about your family
And the things you are able to change,
Continue to live life to its fullest,
Have fun, and make plans that vary in range.

*Your future's already written,*
*You've already been dealt your cards,*
*What matters is how you play them*
*Making your life easy or hard.*

*Don't focus on the negative,*
*Don't dwell on what's not meant to be,*
*Make the best of your situation,*
*Stay positive, and smile:*
*Things will work out,*
*You'll see.*

Kathleen Downing Melillo

*Now It's time to look inward*
*deep down in your soul*
*your future begins*
*when you decide upon your goal*
*Will it be the turning of a page*
*a new chapter or new book*
*is the choice you have to make*
*set the tone early with a clever hook*
*Your happiness awaits*
*you've paid your dues*
*You win or lose*
*by the choices you choose.*

*The choices
we make in life
not the one's made for fun
they determine our character
they make us
not only who we are
but also what we will become.
Choices,
life is full of them,
we make them every day
whether they're
as simple as
what should I have for breakfast
or
what should I wear today.
Think about who you are
or who you want to be;
wake up every day
think about the choices
that lay before you*

*think before you choose*
*it's your future at stake*
*there are many options to weigh.*
*Makes choices for you*
*and for those*
*in your life that really matter*
*because when you think about*
*what's really important*
*the answers are clear*
*they'll be filtered*
*from the background of clatter.*
*Your dreams are yours*
*your course is up to you*
*each decision is your choice*
*be flexible but strong;*
*write your future*
*paint your destiny*
*live your life*
*listen to your own voice.*

*Your past has brought you
to where you stand today
know everything happens for a reason
it's your future,
press play.*

Kathleen Downing Melillo

*Life is complicated
with its twists
and turns,
you've only to
accept your fate
and move on;
never dwell
as it doesn't
change your reality.
The life you've led
until now
is filled with memories,
some cherished,
others
fondly dismissed.
Look toward
your next adventure
with open eyes,
you've lived
and learned,
use this knowledge*

*to see
who you are,
what you want,
and
what the world
has to offer.
You've been given the opportunity
to choose your destination,
so ask yourself
what is it you want
in this new chapter,
how can you incorporate
your old life with the new,
how will you treasure your past,
deal with the present,
and how you can forgive
in order to find the happiness waiting for you.*

Kathleen Downing Melillo

*It's been a quite a trip
one that certainly wasn't planned
after juggling every human emotion possible
I now know on two feel I'll land.*

*Running,
spinning,
whirlwind...
foolish,
thoughtless,
reckless...
crazy,
misguided,
confused...
laughing,
happy,
facade...
drifting,
wandering,
rootless...
seeking,
searching,
quest...
thinking,
feeling,
pondering...
questioning,
doubting,
unsure...
pretend,
phony,
sham...
fearful,
anxious,
convoluted...
off course,
adrift,
lost...
but now I'm found.*

Kathleen Downing Melillo

*I guess I've always been a dreamer*
*an optimist to the core*
*although my optimism has faltered*
*I always knew, for me, that somewhere there'd be more.*

*Sometimes
when I dream
I am
somewhere
over the rainbow...
It's a place
where
beauty exists
in every way...
Each and every
sunrise
is breathtaking...
Days
are sunny and bright
and
there's never
a cloud
in the sky...
Smiles and laughter
are abound*

*and
stress and worry
simply
don't exist...
Flowers
are in perpetual bloom,
and the grass is
always greener
on the other side...
Peace,
tranquility,
and
serenity
exist in
and among
every living being...
Conflict,
hostilities,
and
war
are unknown;
love and life
co-exist...*

*Notice, I never mentioned
About having a man in my life
That's for another chapter
I think I'll call it,
Why I'm Still Not a Wife!*

*On second thought
I'm thinking of book # 2
and it's title,
Why is it taking so long
To finally find you?*

## SOUL MATE

*My entire life
I have dreamed
of
my perfect soul mate.
I can picture
his smile,
hear
his laughter,
see into
his eyes,
feel the gentleness
of his touch,
and the comfort
and safety
of his embrace.
My love for him
never began
with a spark,
it simply existed
as he has
been a part
of me,
always.*

*Maybe
in another
lifetime
"we"
existed
and
are
destined
to be
soul mates
for all eternity.
You are
the one
who
I
will
wait an eternity
to find...*

# ABOUT THE AUTHOR

*Kathy Downing Melillo, a native of RI*
*Is from an Irish catholic family, the last of seven*
*Her mom now heads the Downing clan*
*While her dad watches over all of them from heaven.*

*She's a graduate of Rhode Island College*
*With a bachelors in elementary Ed*
*She's been teaching 4th grade since 2002*
*And for 14 years she was formally wed.*

*She has two girls of her own*
*Abbie and Allie are 19 & 22*
*She's worked hard to make them proud*
*For them, all her heartache, she muddled through.*

*A softball player for the past 40 years*
*She's a well-know third baseman*
*Her teammates are her summer family*
*Playing till she's no longer able is her master plan.*

*She's been writing poems for friends and family*
*For about 30 years*
*And can turn any thought into a poem*
*To elicit a smile or bring about a tear.*

*This is the first book she's published*
*But promises there'll be more*
*For she never stops thinking*
*She's already working on her encore!*